CRIME
SCENE CLUES

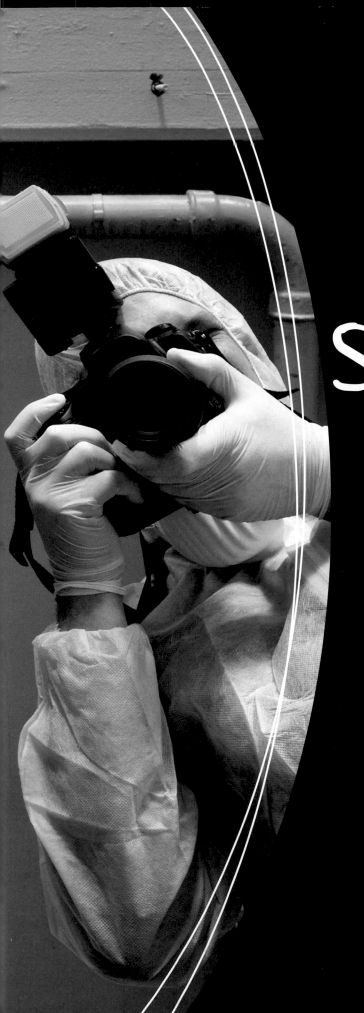

Richard Spilsbury

WAYLAND

First published in 2015 by Wayland
Copyright Wayland 2015

Dewey number: 363.2'5-dc23
ISBN: 9780750294621
10 9 8 7 6 5 4 3 2 1

MIX
Paper from
responsible sources
FSC® C104740
www.fsc.org

Commissioning editor: Victoria Brooker
Project editor: Kelly Davis
Designer: Paul Cherrill for Basement68
Picture research: Richard Spilsbury
and Alice Harman
Proofreader and indexer: Alice Harman

Produced for Wayland by
White-Thomson Publishing Ltd

www.wtpub.co.uk

+44 (0)843 2087 460

Wayland
An imprint of
Hachette Children's Group
Part of Hodder & Stoughton
Carmelite House
50 Victoria Embankment
London EC4Y 0DZ

Printed in China

An Hachette UK company
www.hachette.co.uk
www.hachettechildrens.co.uk

Contents

The scale of things

Many crimes are solved using evidence that you or I can't even see. This is because **forensic scientists** use powerful microscopes to zoom in on evidence so they can study it.

Invisible world

It's hard to imagine how small some things really are. The smallest objects the human eye can see are about 0.2 mm long. There are 1000 **microns** to a millimetre. A human hair (with a width of about 100 microns) is huge, compared to most things scientists zoom in on!

Sense of scale

A scale tells you how big something is shown, compared to its real size. When an image is said to be 25x, that means it's 25 times larger than actual size. You'll see scales next to many images in this book, to give you a sense of the size of objects.

If an adult man was 130 times bigger than actual size, he would be as tall as Big Ben in London!

This flea is **130 TIMES** its actual size

Tools of the trade

How can we zoom in on things? Light **microscopes** bounce light off surfaces to create images. They use **lenses** (curved pieces of glass) that bend light rays to **magnify** an image. The most powerful light microscopes can magnify things up to about 2000 times!

CSIs collect evidence that forensic scientists study under microscopes.

We can use a light microscope to see things that are normally invisible to us.

Forensic fact

Forensic scientists examine **evidence**. The evidence is carefully collected by police or specialist **crime scene investigators (CSIs)**.

Scanning electron microscopes (SEMs)

These microscopes use electrons instead of light. Electrons are tiny parts inside **atoms**. SEMs bounce electrons off surfaces to create images. Electron microscopes can magnify things by almost a million times!

Unique fingerprints

When criminals touch things, they often leave an invisible trail. Traces of sweat or oil in their skin leave an image of the patterns of ridges on their fingertips. Fingerprints lead to many arrests!

Peculiar patterns

No two people have exactly the same fingerprint pattern – not even identical twins! In each fingerprint, the arrangement of ridges is different. For example, there are some areas with loops and others with spirals.

A magnifying glass reveals the unique patterns in a fingerprint.

First find your fingerprint...

Fingers with substances like ink or blood on them leave visible prints, but most fingerprints are invisible. Investigators have to use **ultraviolet (UV) light** to locate hidden fingerprints. Then they apply a fine powder that sticks to the print, making it visible.

Forensic fact

Shining ultraviolet or UV light on fingerprints makes the chemicals they contain glow faintly. CSIs use UV-sensitive cameras to see the prints more easily.

An investigator dusts a fingerprint.

The speed of computers

Police used to have to look through thousands of samples to find a match for a fingerprint. Today they take a close-up photo, and use an electronic fingerprint detector to see if it matches the prints of someone on their database.

Computer software scans the image of the fingerprint to find and mark details that help make it unique, like the points at which ridges meet or cross. Then the computer converts this information into a digital file, and searches rapidly through millions of digital fingerprint records to find a match.

Crime in close-up

In the 1930s, American gangster John Dillinger burnt his fingerprints off his hand with acid. But the fingerprints that grew back on his fingers were identical to the ones he had tried to destroy – and they were used to identify him as the famous killer and bank robber.

High-speed computer fingerprint searches are accurate 99% of the time!

Fingerprints on file

The US Federal Bureau of Investigation (FBI) has more than 450 million fingerprints in its master database of criminal files! Police officers take new fingerprints every time they arrest a suspect.

Hairy hints

A single strand of hair can help to solve a crime! CSIs are more likely to find hairs at the scene of a crime than any other evidence, so how can hairs help them identify the guilty person?

It's in the bag!

CSIs use a **magnifying lamp** to find hair samples at a crime scene. Then they brush the hairs onto a sheet of white paper. Sometimes they put fabric inside a bag and shake it to collect the hairs. They rarely use tweezers — these can damage the hair and ruin the evidence.

Hair-raising crimes

Hair is a great crime-buster! It absorbs chemicals from the bloodstream so it can tell you if someone was poisoned and how much was used.

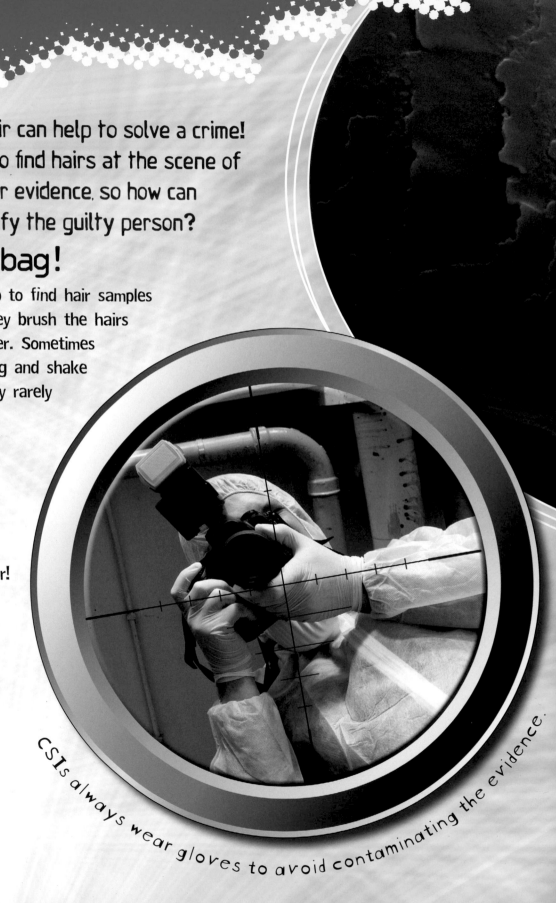

CSIs always wear gloves to avoid contaminating the evidence.

This hair is
2850 TIMES
its actual size

Is it human?

Forensic scientists use a high-powered light microscope to check if a hair is human. Human and animal hairs look different when you zoom in on them. The **cuticle** scales on animal hair are more jagged.

Microscopic roof tiles

The outer layer of a hair is called a cuticle. It is made up of lots of tiny scales. Under a microscope, you can see that the scales on a human hair are flat and overlapping, like roof tiles.
A human hair is the same colour all over. Once they know a hair is human, police can use it to find suspects who have hair the same colour and length.

Forensic fact

Did you know about 100 hairs fall out of a person's head every day?

Secret cells

How can forensic scientists identify someone from traces of spit left on a glass? The secret is in the **cells**.

Where are the cells from?

Cells naturally rub off our bodies every day. Cheek cells rub off the inside of the mouth, and more grow to take their place. We swallow some and some get into our **saliva** (spit). When we drink, some cheek cells may stick to the glass. CSIs rub damp swabs on the glass to collect the cells.

A CSI looks for traces of DNA evidence.

An investigator takes a sample of cheek cells.

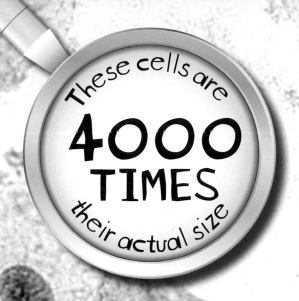

These cells are **4000 TIMES** their actual size

These cheek cells have been magnified under a light microscope.

DNA profiling

Forensic scientists find out who the cells belong to through **DNA profiling**. DNA is an amazing chemical found in cells. It contains 'instructions' about how living things grow and develop. Patterns within these instructions are unique to an individual, rather like fingerprints.

Forensic scientists use chemical tests to compare the DNA patterns in the cells they find with those taken from the mouths of suspects. If the patterns match, it helps prove that the suspect was at the crime scene.

Crime in close-up

In 1985, Kirk Bloodsworth was sent to jail in the USA for murdering a girl, after five eyewitnesses saw him near where she was killed. Seven years later, forensic scientists used new DNA profiling methods to prove that DNA from cells at the crime scene did not match Bloodsworth's. He was finally set free.

Forensic fact

You, like everyone else, normally lose about 1000 cheek cells each day!

13

Glassy giveaways

A broken window at a burglary leaves a shattering mess! But forensic scientists can use the broken glass to help solve the crime.

Collecting the evidence

Investigators collect glass chips at the crime scene, using tweezers or brushes. They store the glassy evidence in sealed tubes or bags. They also look for tiny chips on suspects' clothing or bodies. These may have got there when the criminal broke the window.

Chips

Forensic scientists study the glass chip samples using magnifying glasses and light microscopes. They compare the shapes the glass has broken into, the thickness and colour of the chips, and any surface scratches. They also shine light, to compare differences in the angle in which light is bent as it shines through the glass. A match between samples shows that a suspect broke the window and may have carried out the burglary.

A CSI uses tweezers to collect evidence from a broken window.

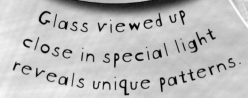

Glass viewed up close in special light reveals unique patterns.

Catching clues

The sharp edges of a broken window can trap clues from criminals, such as scraps of clothing or drops of blood. Forensic scientists can test whether the samples match the clothes or blood type of a suspect.

Forensic fact

Scientists can use powerful **lasers** to produce tiny samples of gas from glass chips. This can help them match different pieces of glass from crime scenes and suspects.

15

Details in the dust

Dust is a lot more interesting than it looks! It is full of all sorts of things, from tiny carpet fibres to skin cells. Forensic scientists zoom in on dust to find lots of clues about crimes.

Dust like this can be made up of almost anything that is small enough to float in air!

A CSI checks clothing for dust particles.

Forensic fact

People shed 30,000–40,000 skin cells per minute, and 75–90% of the dust around us is actually dead skin cells!

A different use for sticky tape!

CSIs have to collect dust very carefully, as it blows away easily. To get dust off a surface like a doorframe or a shirt, they put transparent sticky tape on the surface. Then they peel off the tape, and place it – sticky-side down – on a clean slide, so it can be viewed through a microscope. Sometimes they use a **forensic vacuum** to suck samples of dust from surfaces or hard-to-reach places.

Dissecting dust

Forensic scientists look at dust samples under scanning electron microscopes. They separate particular particles for closer analysis. Particles can identify places or people when they match those at a crime scene. A tiny fibre from a criminal's jumper left at a crime scene can give them away. Kitchen dust, with flour or spices in it, found on that person's jumper, can prove that they were in the victim's house.

pollen grain

cat fur

insect scales

This is a coloured SEM of a sample of household dust. Colouring the different particles makes them easier to see and identify.

synthetic and woollen fibres

This dust sample is **500 TIMES** its actual size

Precious dust?

Dr Edmond Locard set up the world's first forensics laboratory in France in 1910. He proved that dust from clothes worn by suspected **counterfeiters** contained particles of metals that were used to make fake coins.

How plants help police

Pollen is a great crimebuster. These microscopic plant grains cling to suspects' clothes, hair and belongings without them knowing it!

Pollen, pollen everywhere

Pollen gets everywhere. Plants make pollen to be carried by wind or insects to other plants, in order to make seeds. Pollen carried by wind is light, and blows easily into people's hair and clothes. Pollen carried by insects has microscopic hooks or spikes that cling to animals — and people.

Around 240,000 types of plant produce pollen, often in huge quantities.

Powdery yellow pollen clings to a bee's body.

Forensic fact

Pollen grains take a very long time to decay. This is why samples can even be found on **corpses** buried many years before!

This pollen is

6000 TIMES

its actual size

This is an SEM image of pollen from a sunflower.

Zoom in on pollen

Most single pollen grains are invisible to the naked eye, but they have distinctive shapes and colours when you zoom in on them. Scientists use SEMs to view pollen. The image is then linked to a computer database, which matches and identifies the pollen grains. A sample from a criminal or a crime scene will be a unique combination of pollen, depending on plants in the area, weather, season and time of day.

Crime in close-up

In 1996, Michael Bodsworth denied murdering his ex-partner Samantha, whose body was found among flowering wattle trees. But a scientist confirmed that pollen at the crime scene exactly matched pollen found in his car. He was jailed for life.

19

Suspect soil

A stolen car is found in a muddy field, and the person suspected of stealing it has soil on their boots. How do forensic scientists confirm that the suspect was in the car?

Suspect soil

Soil from a crime scene can be compared with soil samples found on the suspect or their belongings. If they match, that means the suspect was there!

Soil can show who committed a crime.

Sorting soil

Soil is partly made up of tiny pieces of rock, so scientists check to see if samples contain the same **minerals**. They also compare colour and the variety and size of the particles. Soil has other things in it too, like bits of dead leaves and animal waste, as well as microscopic worms and other living things.

Soil reveals secrets because soil in one place differs from soil in another.

Singular soil

Each soil sample has a slightly different percentage of minerals, living things and water. They also differ, depending on the weather in a particular area, or whether the soil is found on a hill or on flat ground.

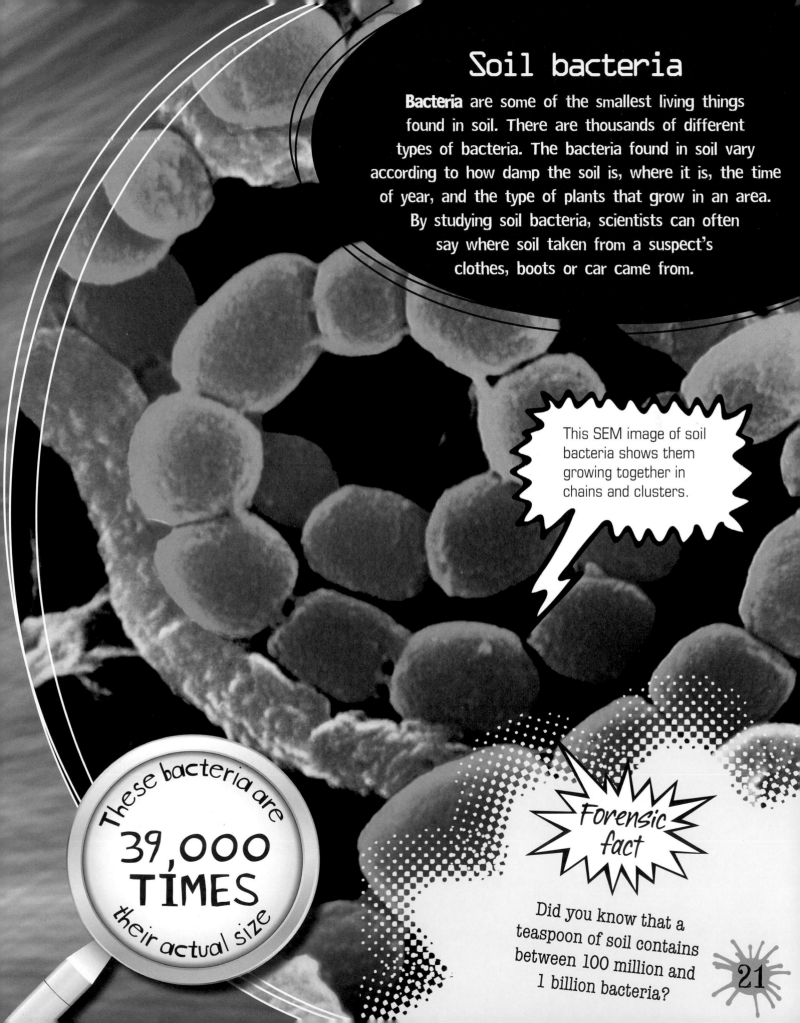

Soil bacteria

Bacteria are some of the smallest living things found in soil. There are thousands of different types of bacteria. The bacteria found in soil vary according to how damp the soil is, where it is, the time of year, and the type of plants that grow in an area. By studying soil bacteria, scientists can often say where soil taken from a suspect's clothes, boots or car came from.

This SEM image of soil bacteria shows them growing together in chains and clusters.

These bacteria are **39,000 TIMES** their actual size

Forensic fact

Did you know that a teaspoon of soil contains between 100 million and 1 billion bacteria?

21

Watery grave

When a dead body is washed up on a riverbank, police have the gruesome job of finding out whether the person drowned. Forensic scientists can help by studying **diatoms** from the water that get into the body.

Different diatoms

Some of the commonest microscopic living things in water are diatoms. There are many different types of diatoms, and they can be identified by their distinctive shapes. Some types live only in fresh water, others just in oceans. Some prefer cold, and others like warm water.

Police divers search for clues in the water.

Diatom clues

CSIs collect samples of diatoms from the water where the body was found. They then look in the lungs, blood, bones and other body parts for diatoms. Diatoms found in the body prove that the person drowned — because they must have been alive to breathe in water, and for their blood to transport diatoms around their body. If the diatom types from the water sample and the body match, then the person drowned where the body was found.

Diatoms come in many different shapes and patterns.

Crime in close-up

In 1991, two boys were attacked and left to drown, but they escaped. Forensic analysis of their clothes and the shoes of several suspects revealed matching diatoms. This evidence showed that the suspects had been at the crime scene.

Forensic fact

About 1000 diatoms could fit inside this 'o'!

Maggot attack

Wriggling maggots can reveal secrets. Forensic scientists can work out when someone died by looking at the maggots and other insects that come to feed on the body.

A disgusting dinner!

Insects feed on the bodies of dead animals. Flies are attracted to the smell of body fluids and gases released by a corpse as it decays. They lay their eggs on corpses so that the maggots that hatch out of them can feed on the bodies. The maggots feed and grow on the corpse until they become adult insects.

The head of a bluebottle fly maggot.

Forensic fact

Blowflies can smell a corpse from 16 km (10 miles) away!

This maggot is **130 TIMES** its actual size

Maggots can reveal how long a body has been dead.

Fly clock

Forensic scientists can work out the time of death by studying the flies on a corpse. If there are lots of eggs, or small, young maggots, then the death was more recent than if lots of older maggots are found. Different types of fly arrive at corpses at different times. For example, blowflies may arrive within minutes to feed on saliva or blood, but cheese flies prefer a more rotted corpse of three to six months old.

Maggots feed on a pig's dead body.

Crime in close-up

In 1986, a murdered woman was found at the side of a road, and CSIs collected 4000 maggots from the corpse. Scientists identified the maggots as blowflies, around seven days old. This helped police find out that a male suspect had been seen where the victim lived, just before her death. This information was used to prove he was guilty.

A maggot nursery

Scientists identify eggs or maggots by zooming in with a scanning electron microscope. Or they sometimes raise maggots in cages and wait for them to turn into adult flies, which are easier to identify.

close to the bone

Forensic scientists can study a skeleton and say how a person died, when they died, and what they ate.

Making a murderous mark

Skeletons of murder victims may carry gruesome tell-tale marks. Someone who was stabbed may have scratch marks or chips removed from bones. Someone who was shot may have shattered bones or a round hole left by a bullet.

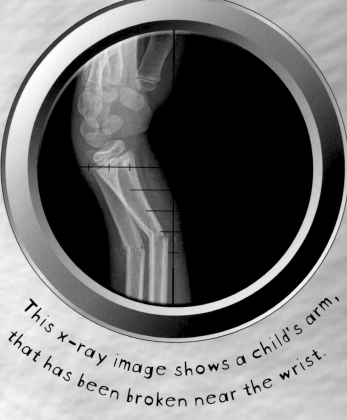

This x-ray image shows a child's arm, that has been broken near the wrist.

Investigators can learn a great deal from the bones of victims.

Old bones?

Looking closely at bones also gives us clues about age. A baby's skeleton is made of smaller, softer bones than that of an adult. As they grow, some of the small bones join up into bigger bones, while soft **cartilage** mostly turns to hard, strong bone. Forensic scientists use **x-ray** machines to look at bone structure. They can tell, for example, whether a skeleton is a teenager or an adult, according to the thickness of cartilage and bone at the ends of the thigh bones.

Toothy clues

The shapes of teeth, their position in the jaw and any fillings or other dental repairs are unique to each individual. Forensic scientists sometimes identify a skull by matching the dental pattern with dental records. They also look closely at the surfaces of the teeth to spot the age.

Enamel grows on teeth in ridges. Zooming in on a tooth's surface allows scientists to spot wear more easily.

Dental wear and tear

Enamel (the hard surface coating on our teeth) wears away gradually as we get older. Looking at enamel wear gives an idea of how old the person was when they died.

Forensic fact

Teeth can survive fierce fires that destroy many other kinds of evidence, including human bones.

Glossary

atom one of the tiny particles that make up everything in the world

bacteria tiny living things that exist in air, water, soil and other living creatures

cartilage strong white substance in the body that stops bones rubbing together

cell the smallest, most basic unit from which all living things are made

corpse dead body

counterfeiter someone who makes fake coins and bank notes

crime scene investigator (CSI) someone who collects evidence from a crime scene

cuticle outer layer of a hair, made up of lots of tiny scales

diatoms tiny living things found in water

DNA profiling method of matching DNA from human cells in order to identify criminals

evidence an object or piece of information that shows whether or not something is true

forensic scientist person who examines evidence

forensic vacuum portable and powerful vacuum cleaner that sucks up tiny particles, to be studied by forensic scientists

laser device that makes and controls a very powerful light beam

lens curved piece of glass that bends light rays; used in microscopes and magnifying glasses

magnify make bigger; enlarge

magnifying glass lens that you hold in your hand, which makes things look bigger

magnifying lamp magnifying glass with a lamp attached to it, to help us see tiny things more easily

micron unit of measurement equal to one-millionth of a metre; 50 microns is about half the width of a human hair

microscope device that produces enlarged images of objects that are normally too small to be seen

microscopic something so small that it can only be seen through a microscope

mineral non-living substance that is naturally found in the earth, such as salt or granite

particle very tiny piece of something

pollen fine powder, usually yellow, that forms in flowers and is carried to other flowers by insects, to make those flowers produce seeds

saliva spit; liquid in the mouth

ultraviolet (UV) light form of light ray in the air that we cannot see

x-ray form of light ray in the air that we cannot see, but that can be used to make images of the bones inside the human body

Find out more

Books

Forensic Science: Collecting Crime-scene Evidence by Carol Ballard (Watts, 2010)
Forensic Science: Identifying Criminals and Victims by Carol Ballard
Forensic Science: Solving Crimes from the Past by Richard Spilsbury
Forensic Science: Solving Crimes in the Lab by Carol Ballard

Graphic Forensic Science: Solving Crimes with Trace Evidence by Gary Jeffrey (Watts, 2009)
Graphic Forensic Science: Crime Scene Investigators by Rob Shone (Watts, 2009)

Inside Crime: Forensics by Colin Hynson (Watts, 2010)

Radar: Police Forensics by Adam Sutherland (Wayland, 2012)

The Impact of Science and Technology: Crime Fighting by Anne Rooney (Watts, 2009)

Websites

www.cyberbee.com/whodunnit/crime.html
and www.wonderville.ca/asset/csi-techniques are both sites that will help you develop
some forensic skills of your own. These include taking fingerprints, analysing mystery
powders and splashes, and measuring footprints in order to work out height.

www.forensicscience.org/resources/forensics-for-kids/
has links to many fascinating forensic science websites, puzzles, games and activities.

Index

Zoom In On

Contents of titles in the series

WAYLAND